Hiking and Camping

The World's Top Hikes and Camping Spots

by Paul Mason

CAPSTONE PRESS
a capstone imprint

Edge Books are published by
Capstone Press, a Capstone imprint,
151 Good Counsel Drive, P.O. Box 669,
Mankato, Minnesota 56002.
www.capstonepub.com

First published 2011
Copyright © 2011 A & C Black
Publishers Limited

Produced for A & C Black by
Monkey Puzzle Media Ltd,
11 Chanctonbury Road,
Hove BN3 6EL, UK

Printed and bound in China by C&C Offset
Printing Co., Ltd.

032011
006117ACF11

The right of Paul Mason to be identified as
the author of this Work has been asserted by
him in accordance with the Copyright, Designs,
and Patents Act 1988.

Library of Congress Cataloging-in-Publication
Data
Mason, Paul, 1967-
    Hiking and camping : the world's top hikes
and camping spots / by Paul Mason.
        p. cm. -- (Edge books: passport to world
sports)
    Includes index.
    ISBN 978-1-4296-6863-7 (library binding)
    1. Hiking--Juvenile literature. 2. Camping--
Juvenile literature. I. Title. II. Series.

    GV199.52.M373 2011
    796.5--dc22

    2011005319

Editor: Dan Rogers
Design: Mayer Media
Picture research: Lynda Lines

This book is produced using paper that
is made from wood grown in managed,
sustainable forests. It is natural, renewable,
and recyclable. The logging and manufacturing
processes conform to the environmental
regulations of the country of origin.

Picture acknowledgements
Action Images p. 8 (Axiom/Zuma Press);
Alamy pp. 4 (Chris Cheadle), 6 (Hawaii Photo
Resource), 9 (Ashley Cooper), 10 (SCPhotos),
12 (The National Trust Photolibrary), 13
(Stuart Forster), 14 (John Warburton-Lee
Photography), 18 (Mediacolor's), 22–23
(Jörg Müller), 25 (Photoshot), 26 (Robert
Preston), 28 (Alex Ekins), 29 (Peter Raven/Mark
Custance); Corbis pp. 5 (Stefanie Grewel), 7
(Anthony West), 20 (Whit Richardson); Florida
Trail Association p. 16 (Robert Coveney);
iStockphoto pp. 15, 27; Paul Mason p. 17;
Photolibrary pp. 1 (Bill Stevenson), 11 (Bill
Stevenson), 21 (Bill Stevenson/Superstock), 23
top (John Warburton-Lee Photography), 24
(Robert Harding Travel/Christopher Rennie);
Wikimedia pp. 18–19, 19 top. Compass rose
artwork on front cover and inside pages by
iStockphoto. Map artwork by MPM Images.

The front cover shows a hiker by his campfire
in the Chugach State Park, Alaska (Alamy/
Alaska Stock).

SAFETY ADVICE

Don't attempt any of the
activities or techniques
in this book without the
guidance of a qualified
guide or instructor.

CONTENTS

It's a Wild World

Imagine sleeping in your tent, wrapped up warm and cozy in a sleeping bag. You're surrounded by the sounds of nature—the wind in the trees or gentle surf on a beach. You wake at dawn, unzip the tent, and enjoy the sunrise. Hiking and camping can take you there!

THE WORLD OF HIKING AND CAMPING

Hiking gets us away from the world most people live in—the world of cars and concrete, noise, and pollution. Just an hour's hike can take you out into nature. You might spot anything from a bear to a tiny dormouse! Camping adds the fun of an overnight trip.

What a great place to wake up! Hiking and camping can take you to some of the world's most beautiful—and peaceful—places.

PASSPORT TO HIKING AND CAMPING

Everything you need to know about hiking and camping is gathered together in this book. Even better, you can find out about some of the best hiking trails and camping spots in the world. But you might need to save up for a while to get to some of them. Hiking and camping don't have to be expensive, though. Basic equipment can be quite inexpensive, and there's certain to be somewhere to visit not far from your home.

THE SECRET LANGUAGE OF HIKING

Hiking does not require lots of equipment. The most important things are good places to walk and good friends to walk with.

terrain type of ground, e.g. rocky, steep, flat, etc.
thermal to do with heat. Thermal underwear helps keep you warm.

Technical: Hiking checklist

Before going on a hike, make sure you are taking the right clothing and equipment with you. Exactly what to take depends on the **terrain**, the temperature, and how far you are going, but here are a few basics:

Warm-weather/summer hiking:

• Comfortable walking boots or shoes and comfortable socks (special hiking socks have padded toes and heels).

• Loose or stretchy clothing.

• A warm layer and a waterproof top.

• Plenty of water and food if you are going to be walking for over an hour.

• A hat and sunscreen.

• A map and a cell phone with emergency numbers.

For cold weather, take everything you would take in summer, plus:

• A warm hat and gloves.

• An extra warm layer and possibly **thermal** underwear.

• Always wear long pants.

• In snowy conditions, wear sunglasses to protect your eyes.

Na Pali Coast

The Hawaiian island of Kauai would be a great place to head for your first-ever hike. The temperature rarely drops below 61° Fahrenheit (16° Celsius), even at night. And in summer, anything more than a light shower of rain is unusual. One of the most beautiful parts of the island is the Na Pali coast.

NA PALI COAST
Location: Hawaii
Type of hike: coastal
Difficulty level: 1 of 5
Best season: May to October

HIKING THE NA PALI COAST

The Na Pali coast is made up of *pali*, or cliffs, broken up by narrow valleys and a few beautiful beaches. Hikers can follow the Kalalau Trail, an ancient path originally built by native Hawaiians to reach their terraced fields. A good one-day walk on the trail goes between the beaches at Ke'e and Hanikapi'ai, and back.

Great views along the northwestern coast of Kauai, Hawaii

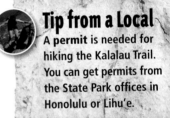

Tip from a Local
A **permit** is needed for hiking the Kalalau Trail. You can get permits from the State Park offices in Honolulu or Lihu'e.

TECHNIQUE
Travel light

Clothes for a week? Check. Skis and ski boots? Check. Teddy bear? Of course!

ESSENTIAL INFORMATION

Whatever time of year, the air temperature is almost never uncomfortably high or low in Hawaii. In winter, though, heavy rainfall can be unpleasant and make the trail slippery.

Clothing: Travel light, but always take rain gear, even in summer, in case of a shower.

Other equipment: Mosquito repellent will definitely be useful in the evenings.

Hazards: Be careful of the ocean at Hanikapi'ai, as the surf and currents here can be very strong.

If you like Na Pali ...

you could also try:
- Abel Tasman Coast Track, New Zealand
- Lycian (pronounced "lick-ee-an") Way, Turkey

Deciding what to take on a hike can be difficult. If you take too much, the extra weight could spoil your day. But so could searching in your bag for a rain jacket, only to find you left it at home! Here are a few tips:

• You will warm up after a few minutes of walking. If you are the perfect temperature when you begin, you will probably soon be too hot. Maybe you could lose a layer?

• Never scrimp on water or food. Experts recommend people drink at least 4.2–6.3 pints (2–3 liters) of water a day. You should drink more when doing hard exercise or in hot weather. When going away for days, water-**purifying** tablets may come in handy.

The South Downs Way

The South Downs is home to some classic English countryside. The Way starts in the ancient city of Winchester. It crosses the rolling countryside and farmland of Hampshire and Sussex and ends at the white, chalky cliffs near Eastbourne on the south coast.

HIKING THE SOUTH DOWNS WAY

The entire route is 100 miles (160 kilometers) long. That's much too far for a single day's hiking. Most people hike along a shorter section of the route. With plenty of train stations, bus stops, and cafés, it's easy to plan a day's hike anywhere between Winchester and Eastbourne.

THE SOUTH DOWNS
Location: Hampshire/Sussex, England
Type of hike: coastal
Difficulty level: 1.5 of 5
Best season: May to September

The South Downs Way is one of Britain's most popular long-distance trails. It passes through some of the most beautiful countryside in Southern England.

Tip from a Local
The Devil's Dyke is beside the South Downs Way. It is a steep-sided valley and is said to have been dug by the Devil, as part of his plan to drown a nearby village.

If you like the South Downs Way ...

you could also try:
• The Loire Valley Trail, France
• Tahoe Rim Trail, California/ Nevada

THE SECRET LANGUAGE OF HIKING

tops high ground at the top of a hill or mountain

escape finish a hike early because something has gone wrong

ESSENTIAL INFORMATION

The best chance of good weather is in summer. But in England, it can rain at any time of year. In winter snowfall occasionally makes the Downs look more like Lapland.

Clothing: In summer light clothing and shoes are fine. In winter it can be very cold and windy up on the exposed **tops**.

Other equipment: A map covering the section you are walking will make an **escape** easier, if the weather turns bad.

TECHNIQUE
Following the trail markers

Where there's a choice of routes, it's not always easy to find your way even if there are trail signs. It's always a good idea to carry a map of the area with you.

Many official hiking routes are marked out to make them easier to follow. Following a marked trail is a great way to get into hiking. It makes it much harder to get lost.

• Follow the direction markers carefully. If you miss one, you may have to retrace your steps. Sometimes the signs show more than one route. Always double check you are following the right one in the right direction!

• Take a map of the route with you as a backup. Usually these can either be downloaded from the Internet, collected at a visitor center, or bought from a store.

The John Muir Trail

The John Muir Trail is regularly voted one of the top 10 hiking trails anywhere in the world. It winds its way through some of North America's most beautiful scenery. The trail starts in the Yosemite National Park and finishes 153 miles (246 kilometers) later at Mount Witney.

THE JOHN MUIR TRAIL
Location: California
Type of hike: mixed
Difficulty level: 2 of 5
Best season: June to September

Setting up camp for the night at a high spot on the John Muir Trail

THE SECRET LANGUAGE OF HIKING

bear canister airtight container for food. It stops food smells from reaching hungry bears' nostrils.

Tip from a Local
John Muir (1838–1914) was a Scottish-American who campaigned for the protection of the United States' wilderness areas.

If you like the John Muir Trail ...
you could also try:
- The Overland Track, Tasmania, Australia
- Alta Via (High Way) number 1, Italy

High above the Yosemite Valley, a hiker takes in the view.

HIKING THE JOHN MUIR TRAIL

Hiking the whole trail at once takes most people up to a month. It is easy to do sections of the trail that take as little as a day. From Yosemite Valley, the trail passes through the Ansel Adams Wilderness, Sequoia National Park, and Kings Canyon National Park.

WEATHER AND EQUIPMENT

The trail is probably best in summer, when lightweight gear should be suitable for day-long walks. At other times of year, the weather and temperature can change rapidly, meaning rain gear and warm clothes may be needed. Anyone sleeping overnight on the trail will need **bear canisters** to stop bears from prowling into camp at night looking for food.

The Lake District

The wild beauty of the Lake District has inspired famous poets such as William Wordsworth and artists such as John Ruskin. When you hike or camp in the Lake District, you are probably visiting the most famous countryside in Britain and maybe even the world.

THE LAKE DISTRICT
Location: Cumbria, England
Type of hike: mixed
Difficulty level: 2 of 5
Best season: May, June and September

HIKING IN THE LAKE DISTRICT

Many hikers come to **the Lakes** to climb the high mountains, or "fells." These include Scafell Pike, the highest peak in England, and Helvellyn. The classic route to Helvellyn runs along Striding Edge, a narrow path along a sharp **arête**. There are also many beautiful walks along the sides of the lakes.

If you don't like the weather in the Lake District, wait half an hour. Up in the mountains, weather changes very quickly.

Tip from a Local
Bassenthwaite Lake is the only official "lake" in the Lake District. All the rest are known as either "mere" or "water."

Technical: Tents and sleeping bags

If you are camping out, you will only get a good night's sleep if your tent keeps you dry, and your sleeping bag keeps you warm.

• Tents with an inner and outer layer are best. The outer layer keeps out rain. The inner will have a groundsheet sewn in to keep you off wet ground, and stop ants from crawling into your sleeping bag.

• Sleeping bags are rated for warmth, usually by season. A 1- or 2-season bag is for summer only. A 3-season bag is good for everything except cold weather, and 4-season is for winter.

• Never pitch your tent in a hollow or on low ground. If it rains, that will be the first place to flood. If you get cold at night, wearing a hat will warm you up.

Always try to find a level spot for your tent. Otherwise everyone ends up rolling to one side during the night!

If you like the Lake District ...

you could also try:
• The Lakes Area, New Hampshire
• Mziki Hiking Trail, South Africa

ESSENTIAL INFORMATION

Whatever time of year you visit, there's a good chance it will rain. The warmest months are June to September. But during the summer vacation, the Lakes can be very crowded.

Clothing: Always bring rain gear and a warm top, even in summer. At any other time of year, cold-weather clothes will be needed.

Other equipment: Take a map of the area, and a cell phone with the mountain-rescue number stored in its memory.

Hazards: Sudden storms, ice or snow during winter.

The Blue Mountains

For years after Europeans first arrived in Australia, the Blue Mountains were a barrier they were unable to cross. They did finally break through, and today the area is criss-crossed by some amazing trails (as well as roads and railroad tracks).

THE BLUE MOUNTAINS
Location: New South Wales, Australia
Type of hike: mixed
Difficulty level: 2.5 of 5
Best season: all year round

Tip from a Local

Leave details of your route and what time you expect to get back with a responsible adult. He or she can raise the alarm if you don't show up.

A family hiking through Leura Forest on the Federal Pass. This is one of many trails through the Blue Mountains.

Hiking the Blue Mountains

The Blue Mountains has a fantastic variety of trails. In one hike, you can find yourself gazing out from a high **escarpment** and working your way down a steep rock face. Then you could be picking your way along a gully that wouldn't be out of place in a dinosaur movie.

The Secret Language of Hiking

escarpment inland place where high ground ends in a cliff

Essentail information

Hiking is possible all year round in the Blue Mountains. In summer (January to March), it can be extremely hot, and many people think spring and autumn are the best times to visit.

Clothing: Warm-weather gear is usually enough, plus a warm top and a rain jacket.

Other equipment: Take plenty of water, a map, and a compass.

Hazards: Australia is full of natural hazards, including poisonous snakes and spiders.

TECHNIQUE
Map reading

Binoculars or a monocular are sometimes useful for identifying landmarks shown on a map.

Every year, people get into danger in the Blue Mountains because they get lost. The area is very wild, and if you lose the established trails it becomes very hard to find your way. Good map reading is an essential skill.

• The best way to use a map is never to lose track of your position on it. Trace the route you're planning to take on the map before you leave on a hike.

• Every time the trail passes a landmark, such as a lake, or the path forks, or you go up or down a steep slope, check the map to see if you are still going the right way.

• If you are unsure, retrace your steps until you find a landmark you know is right. Then start again from there.

If you like the Blue Mountains ...

you could also try:
• The Atlas Mountains, Morocco
• Dartmoor, England

Kissimmee River Trail

Part of the fun of hiking is spotting wildlife you just don't see in the city. This walk through a remote part of Florida offers lots of chances to spot some amazing animals, including cranes, deer, wild turkeys, wild hogs, hawks, alligators, and eagles.

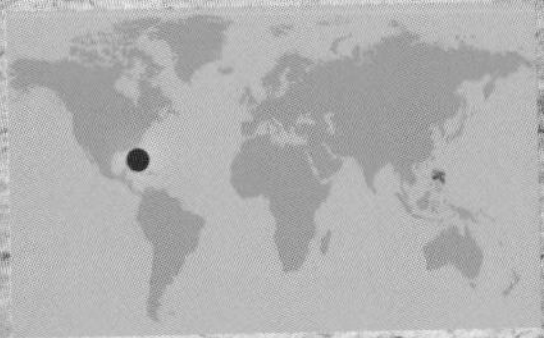

KISSIMMEE RIVER TRAIL
Location: Florida
Type of hike: flat
Difficulty level: 2.5 of 5
Best season: January to April

Tip from a Local
There are 10 campsites along the trail, so it is a good choice for an overnight stop or two.

Along parts of the Kissimmee River Trail, trees provide some welcome shade.

HIKING THE KISSIMMEE RIVER NATIONAL SCENIC TRAIL

This trail runs alongside the Kissimmee River. It is 33.2 miles (53.4 kilometers) long, and is part of the larger Florida Trail, which runs through the state.

The stretch along the Kissimmee River is a relatively easy walk across flat land. Hikers pass through swampland, pine flatlands, and oak **hammocks**.

If you like the Kissimmee River Trail ...

you could also try:
- Derwent River Walk, England
- Lake Waikaremoana Track, New Zealand

ESSENTIAL INFORMATION

The trail can be very wet and is best hiked in the dry season, between January and April.

Clothing: Light clothing is ideal, as the daytime temperature is usually warm or hot all year round.

Other equipment: Bring plenty of water, insect repellent, sunscreen, and a sun hat.

Hazards: Alligators and poisonous snakes live in this area, but rarely cross paths with hikers. The biting insects are also annoying.

THE SECRET LANGUAGE OF HIKING

hammock area of raised ground in a wetland

points of the compass north, south, east, and west

equator imaginary line around the middle of the Earth

TECHNIQUE
Finding your way without a map

This is an easy way to work out the **points of the compass**. It takes about two hours, either side of midday.

1. Push a stick about 12 inches (30 centimeters) long into the ground, pointing straight upward.

2. Every 10 minutes, mark the tip of the stick's shadow with a pebble.

3. Keep doing this until you find yourself putting pebbles further from the stick because the shadow is getting longer.

4. The line from the base of the stick to the nearest pebble will be pointing roughly north-south. South of the **equator**, north is at the stick end. North of the equator, north is at the pebble end.

Finding direction in the wilderness. A line from the stick to the second stone from the left runs roughly south-north.

Kungsleden

Lapland lies in the far north of Sweden. It is so far north that, in summer, it never gets dark here. Crossing this wild territory is the Kungsleden, or "King's Trail." For 264 miles (425 kilometers), the route passes through some of northern Sweden's most breathtaking landscapes.

KUNGSLEDEN
Location: Lapland, Sweden
Type of hike: mixed
Difficulty level: 3 of 5
Best season: May to July

MOUNTAIN LANDSCAPES

From the north, the trail heads south through the Kebnekaise mountain range. These are Sweden's highest mountains. On a clear day, you can see almost a tenth of Sweden from the top of the Kebnekaise. Then the trail runs south again, through more mountains, heading for the Golden Gate.

THE GOLDEN GATE

The Golden Gate lies between the villages of Ammarnäs and Hemavan.

It is a group of islands connected by five suspension bridges and two plank bridges. The scenery here makes a great change from the mountains further north.

STOPPING PLACES

All along the Kungsleden are mountain huts and hostels, where you can unroll your sleeping bag at night and buy food and water. It is easy to hike short sections of the trail for two or three days. It's best to get dropped off at one hut and be picked up from another.

A hiker makes his way carefully over one of the suspension bridges along the Kungsleden.

The *Kungsleden* crosses some of northern
Europe's most remote wilderness.

Tip from a Local

During spring, it is possible
to follow the Kungsleden
on **telemark** skis. It's a
popular trip at Easter.

*Even when snow covers
the ground, a few hardy
cross-country skiers enjoy
following the route.*

If you like the Kungsleden ...

you could also try:
- The Appalachian Trail,
  Eastern United States
- The West Coast Trail, Canada

THE SECRET LANGUAGE OF HIKING

telemark skis that can travel
uphill as well as down
and along flat ground

21

Zion National Park

Zion National Park has something for every kind of hiker. The lower-level paths offer the chance for an easy morning or afternoon walk. Some paths are wheelchair accessible. The higher, more remote tracks will test the skills of even the most experienced hiker.

ZION NATIONAL PARK
Location: Utah
Type of hike: mixed
Difficulty level: 3 of 5
Best season: May, June, September, and October

Over many centuries, water has carved Zion's canyons into eerie shapes.

If you like Zion ...

you could also try:
- **Supramonte Mountains, Sardinia, Italy**
- **Kings Canyon National Park, California**

Tip from a Local

Always take plenty of water into Zion. On most trails, none is available.

Hiking Zion

Zion is famous for its **canyon** hikes, which follow deep, river-cut canyons through the **sandstone**. The most popular of these is The Narrows, a tough, 16-mile (26-kilometer) hike following the Virgin River. The trail passes alongside canyon walls that are 1,970 feet (600 meters) high and in places only 33 feet (10 meters) apart. For the complete experience, camp out at one of the 12 camping spots along the canyon.

Essential information

It is possible to hike in Zion all year. During winter the higher areas can be cold, icy, and snowy. The lower areas are much safer and, for most people, more enjoyable.

Clothing: In summer it is important to protect yourself from the sun and from overheating. Cover up using light, loose clothing and a sun hat.

Other equipment: Definitely put insect repellent and plenty of water in your pack.

Hazards: The canyons can flood during or after heavy rain. If the water gets mucky or starts to rise, find higher ground at least 6.6 feet (2 meters) above the river.

THE SECRET LANGUAGE OF HIKING

canyon steep-sided, narrow river valley

sandstone soft, light-colored type of rock

TECHNIQUE
Cooking safely outdoors

You can easily cook a simple meal on a basic, lightweight gas stove like this one.

Fires are only allowed in some of Zion's official campgrounds. Elsewhere, the risk of fire means only camping stoves may be used. Even when using a stove it is important to be careful.

1. Set up your stove on a hard, level surface such as a flat rock. Have it as far as possible from anything flammable.

2. If your stove uses liquid fuel, pour it in without spilling any, seal the fuel bottle and put it at least a 3 feet (0.9 meters) away.

3. When lighting the stove, make sure that any matches you use are completely put out by dunking them in water.

4. When you have finished cooking, make sure the stove is fully out. Do not leave it unattended until it is cool to the touch.

The Western Isles

In the Western Isles, steep-sided mountains rise up from the sea, inviting you to climb them and enjoy the view. The islands' beaches offer a change of scene, where you can look for otters and seabirds. Or you could just enjoy a picnic lunch on the sand!

HIKING AND CAMPING THE WESTERN ISLES

The Western Isles pack a huge variety of landscapes into a small area. Hiking is made even more attractive by Scotland's "right to roam." This law says that ordinary people are allowed to walk on almost all open land, even if it is privately owned. You are also allowed to camp, in small groups, for two or three nights.

The dramatic, wave-broken coasts of the Western Isles are a hiking paradise (so long as you don't mind wet weather).

THE WESTERN ISLES
Location: Scotland
Type of hike: mixed
Difficulty level: 3 of 5
Best season: May, June, and September

THE SECRET LANGUAGE OF HIKING

day pack small backpack for carrying a day's equipment

scramble hike up a steep slope using both hands and feet

Tip from a Local

For a taste of the Western Isles, visit the island of Arran. It is sometimes known as "Scotland in miniature."

If you like the Western Isles ...

you could also try:
• Vancouver Island, Canada
• Brijuni Islands, Croatia

ESSENTIAL INFORMATION

In May, June, and September, you have the best chance of good weather without the dreaded "midges." These tiny biting insects can become a real pain in summer.

Clothing: In Scotland, there's always the chance of rain and cold weather. Even on the warmest day, pack accordingly.

Other equipment: In summer some people walk in hats with "midge curtains" of fine mesh hanging from the brim.

Hazards: Midges. In winter high winds and heavy rain can cause real danger.

TECHNIQUE
Ascending and descending rough terrain

On some hikes, a bit of near-climbing (called scrambling) is needed.

The steep-sided slopes of the Scottish mountains can be hard work and very tiring to walk up—and down. A few hiking tips can make things easier.

• Never carry more than you need up a mountain. If you are taking a side trip from a long hike, find somewhere to leave your heavy pack and just take a **day pack**.

• When walking uphill or downhill, take lots of small steps instead of a few big ones. It is far less tiring over the course of a long walk.

• Never walk faster than a pace at which you can carry on talking to your friends. If you do, your body will start to use up energy very quickly.

• On steep slopes, use your hands to help you **scramble** upward.

23

The Inca Trail

High up in Peru's Andes Mountains lies the Inca city of Machu Picchu. It was discovered only recently, having been hidden from the world for hundreds of years. Today, hikers can follow an ancient trail that winds up to Machu Picchu through the mountains.

Don't look down! Avoid the trail to Machu Picchu if you're nervous about heights or steep drops!

THE INCA TRAIL
Location: Andes Mountains, Peru
Type of hike: mountainous
Difficulty level: 3.5 of 5
Best season: May to September

Tip from a Local

Watch out for orchids on the trail. You will spot lots of beautiful examples of these rare flowers.

If you like the Inca Trail ...

you could also try:
- The Lares Trail, Peru
- Hadrian's Wall Path, England

Hiking the Inca Trail

There are two main versions of the trail. The first takes four days, and the second takes seven. Both feature breathtaking views of snow-capped mountains and Inca ruins. Having reached Machu Picchu, most hikers walk to the town of Aguas Calientes, which is 3.7 miles (6 kilometers) away. From there, they can catch a train or bus to their next destination.

Essential information

The trail is driest between April and October. In the wet season, between January and March, it can be waterlogged.

Clothing: Travel as light as possible, but be prepared for very hot days and very cold nights.

Other equipment: It's very important to have a warm sleeping bag.

Hazards: It's cold at night and hot during the day. There's a risk of **altitude sickness**.

THE SECRET LANGUAGE OF HIKING

altitude sickness headache, sickness, and confusion caused by high altitude. Unless the sufferer climbs down, it can lead to death.

pack out pack up and take away with you

Always pack out your trash. If you leave yours behind, other people will probably decide it's OK to leave theirs too.

TECHNIQUE
Avoiding trail damage

Hikers in large numbers damage the very landscape they have come to enjoy. The Inca Trail has to close every February so that the damage caused by thousands of hikers can be repaired. Here are some ways to minimize this damage:

• Stick to the trail. When people wander off the trail it creates new paths, wearing away the vegetation and soil.

• Only camp where camping is allowed. It's a good idea to move your tent after a night or two so that the grass underneath it is not damaged.

• **Pack out** what you bring into wilderness areas. Never leave behind trash of any kind, especially plastics or metals that will not decay for many years.

Annapurna Sanctuary

Almost every hiker dreams of one day visiting the Himalayas. This trip offers the chance to trek through the world's highest mountains and visit villages you can only reach on foot. The dramatic scenery and Nepali people make this a hiking paradise.

ANNAPURNA SANCTUARY
Location: Nepal
Type of hike: mountainous
Difficulty level: 4 of 5
Best season: February to May and September to December

LAND OF THE GODS

Annapurna Sanctuary is a high **plateau** surrounded by the Annapurna Mountains. The only way in or out of the Sanctuary is a narrow pass between two peaks. Inside is a land regarded as sacred by the Gurung people. Until 100 years ago, they were the only humans to know the area. The Gurung believed that the Sanctuary was home to many gods, including Shiva, chief of all their gods.

Tip from a Local

The trek to Annapurna Sanctuary is called a **"teahouse** trek." Hikers stay in teahouses, rather than camping, so there's no need to bring a tent.

Flags with prayers printed on them, on the trail to Annapurna Sanctuary. Buddhists believe that as the flags flap in the wind the prayers are carried to heaven.

The view from a teahouse balcony. Imagine waking up and opening your door to this! Teahouses offer hikers food and a place to stay so that they don't need to carry tents.

HIKING TO THE SANCTUARY

The hike usually takes between eight and 10 days, starting from the small town of Nayapul. It follows paths and tracks that wind along the mountainsides, dropping into steep valleys before rising up again. After a whole day's walking you can feel like you haven't actually moved very far! Temperatures vary from very cold at night to extremely hot at midday. A variety of clothes will definitely be needed.

If you like Annapurna Sanctuary ...

you could also try:
- Tongariro Circuit, New Zealand
- Los Glaciares National Park, Argentina

THE SECRET LANGUAGE OF HIKING

plateau flat area of high ground

teahouse mixture of café and hostel found in the Himalayas

Mount Kilimanjaro

Kilimanjaro is not only the highest mountain in Africa but also one of the biggest volcanoes on Earth. It has been 360,000 years since the volcano's last major eruption.

MOUNT KILIMANJARO
Location: Kenya/Tanzania
Type of hike: mountain
Difficulty level: 4 of 5
Best season: January to mid-March and June to October

It might be in Africa, but it still gets snowy and cold at the summit of Mount Kilimanjaro.

Tip from a Local

If potatoes are served for dinner on the first night, don't miss out. They will all be cooked then because they're so heavy to carry!

Information: The Seven Summits

Kilimanjaro is one of the "Seven Summits." These are the highest mountains on each of the Earth's seven continents.

• Kilimanjaro is the only one of the Seven Summits that can be climbed without specialist climbing skills. Mount Kosciusko in Australia is an easy hike, and used to be included in the list.

It has now been replaced by Carstensz Pyramid in Indonesia, which is over twice as high.

• The Vinson Massif would be an easy climb—except for the fact that it's the highest mountain in Antarctica! The freezing temperatures and high winds make it an impossible challenge without specialist equipment.

Climbing Kilimanjaro

Kilimanjaro is 19,341 feet (5,895 meters) above sea level. It is possible to hike to the summit in five to seven days, though you do need to be fit and experienced. There are six main routes to the summit, starting from either Tanzania or Kenya. The easiest routes are Rongai (on which people sleep in tents) and Marangu (with hut-based shelter).

If you like Mt. Kilimanjaro ...
you could also try:
- Mount Kosciusko, Australia
- Ben Nevis, Scotland

Like Kilimanjaro, many mountains have a choice of routes up and down. Experienced hikers always pick the route that will suit the slowest, least-fit member of their group. That way, everyone can hike together.

Essential Information

Kilimanjaro is best climbed during its two dry seasons. Of these, January to March is quieter but colder. June to October is busier but warmer.

Clothing: Shorts and a T-shirt are usually fine during daytime. In the evening and at night the temperature drops and it can be very cold. There is always snow at the summit.

Other equipment: You'll need a sleeping bag, water bottles, purification tablets, sunscreen, and sunglasses.

Hazards: Altitude sickness kills several people each year on Kilimanjaro.

THE SECRET LANGUAGE OF HIKING
summit highest point

Glossary

WORDS FROM THE SECRET LANGUAGE FEATURES

altitude sickness headache, sickness, and confusion caused by high altitude. Unless the sufferer climbs down, it can lead to death.

arête ridge of rock that is steep-sided and narrow at the top

bear canister airtight container for food. It stops food smells from reaching hungry bears' nostrils.

canyon steep-sided, narrow river valley

day pack small backpack for carrying a day's equipment

equator imaginary line around the middle of the Earth

escape finish a hike early because something has gone wrong

escarpment inland place where high ground ends in a cliff

hammock area of raised ground in a wetland

pack out pack up and take away with you

permit piece of paper giving permission

plateau flat area of high ground

points of the compass north, south, east, and west

purifying making clean

sandstone soft, light-colored type of rock

scramble hike up a steep slope using both hands and feet

summit highest point

teahouse mixture of café and hostel found in the Himalayas

telemark skis that can travel uphill, as well as down and along flat ground

terrain type of ground, e.g. rocky, steep, flat, etc.

the Lakes short for the Lake District

thermal to do with heat. Thermal underwear helps keep you warm.

tops areas of high ground at the top of a hill or mountain

OTHER WORDS HIKERS AND CAMPERS USE

bivvy short for "bivouac," meaning an overnight stay where there is little or no shelter

cairn cone of rocks piled up to mark the route of a trail

camel up drink as much water as possible

GPS Global Positioning System, a way of finding your route using a hand-held computer and satellite signals

hiker midnight 9 p.m. (because most hikers are so tired that they're usually fast asleep by then)

potable describes water that it is safe to drink (so, "non-potable" means do NOT drink it)

switchback tight turn in a trail as it goes up or down a steep slope

through hiker someone who is walking the entire length of a long-distance trail

Finding Out More

The Internet

FactHound offers a safe, fun way to find Internet sites related to this book. All of the sites on FactHound have been researched by our staff.

Here's all you do:
Visit www.facthound.com
FactHound will fetch the best sites for you!

Books

Camping and Hiking (Get Outdoors) Neil Champion (PowerKids Press, 2011)

Camping for Fun! (For Fun!) Jana Voelke Studelska (Compass Point Books, 2008)

Hiking (Outdoor Adventures) Gillian Richardson (Weigl Publishers, 2008)

Magazine

Most hiking and outdoor magazines carry a mixture of articles on equipment, personalities, contests, and travel. They all have websites you can locate by searching by name.

Outside
This magazine carries high-quality travel articles, features, and equipment reviews.

Index